James Martineau

Faith the beginning

self-surrender the fulfillment of the spiritual life

James Martineau

Faith the beginning
self-surrender the fulfillment of the spiritual life

ISBN/EAN: 9783741154669

Manufactured in Europe, USA, Canada, Australia, Japa

Cover: Foto ©Andreas Hilbeck / pixelio.de

Manufactured and distributed by brebook publishing software (www.brebook.com)

James Martineau

Faith the beginning

FAITH THE BEGINNING, SELF-SURRENDER THE FULFILMENT, OF THE SPIRITUAL LIFE.

By **James Martineau**, D.D., D.C.L.,
Author of "Endeavours after a Christian Life," "Hours of Thought," &c.

NEW YORK:
THE MACMILLAN CO. 1897.

Contents.

	PAGE
Faith the Root of Knowledge and of Love	1
The Lapse of Time and the Law of Obligation	35
Thou Art My Strength	67
The Claims of Christian Enterprise	97

Faith the Root
of
Knowledge and of Love.

to read off the appearances of life by the light of a pure and loving soul, and repress as a temptation the misgivings of a cold, untrustful temper. *There* we know well enough that as a man feels so will he think; that the scene before him will take its colour from the tint of his affections; yet we do not on that account mock at all his notions as a dream of the insane, or, unless they betray him into manifest illusions, suppose him cut off from all hope of knowing the truth. Nor do we recommend him, in order to prevent mistakes, to get rid of all his affections and become indifferent to every thing now dear. Thus to slip the shades over every luminous side of his moral nature would only turn it into a dark lantern, with which, prowl about as he may, he could find neither knaves nor honest men. Impartiality of this sort—consisting of absolute suppression of every wish—is only another name for utter blindness to the relations of the moral world. Extinguish every emotion, and no intellect remains by which any sense at all can be extracted from the course of human affairs. You might still, indeed, beat time like a clock, and measure space like a chain, and weigh the strength of the winds, and keep account of damps and heat; you might grind your corn and post your books. But with the physical outside and uses of things your intelligence would stop; their expressiveness would lie in the dark; no sound would be music, no sight would be beauty; the eyes of a saint would be but two optical organs, and the sweetest smile but a twisted mouth. Accordingly, there are no men whose judgment on human life is so incompetent, and who pass through it so ignorant of its chief realities, as those who have no heart-wisdom, and, in the numbness of their nature, rely on mere sharp-sightedness for seeing what is invisible. Clear, impartial insight requires, not that we have *no* preferences, but that we have *right* preferences; not that we shut ourselves up with one faculty, but that we be free through the harmony of all. A man who cannot see correctly unless he is perfectly indifferent as to what he sees, to whom one discovery must be as welcome as another else he will lie to his own heart, who cannot give an honest verdict in the face of agony, is unfit for the exercise of moral judgment at all. There is no such thing as mere *outside evidence* of matters either human or Divine. It is all reciprocation and response between the inner soul and the outer object; and the quickness of that response, the penetration of the glance, the certainty of the mutual understanding, will depend not on the coldness, but on the fixed intensity of the mind that sends forth its look. If you carry tidings that a child is dead, the mother will be the first to read the news upon your very face, and drag it from the hiding of your reserve; and if there were no God, the soul that had loved Him most, and could pretend to no joy without His presence, would be the first to miss Him. To say, as some strangely do, that religious people cannot judge about religion, is like saying that the humane cannot understand suffering, or genius appreciate poetry; that for truth in Art you must avoid consulting Raphael, and in music you must keep clear of Beethoven. In contradiction to all such pedantry I venture to maintain that only through love and trust can God be known; that by bare sense and understanding faith may be lost, but can never be won; that when it goes, the intellect is in such relations intellect no more, but is turned from a medium of light to an instrument of delusion and, degraded from the prophet's rod to the measuring staff of material science, ennobles and consecrates us no more. To a being quite strange to our affections—a being differently made and coming from another world—the human countenance would present nothing but a configuration of protuberances and depressions; all the dear living light, the waves of thought that chase across like corn that bends before the wind, the springing tears, the kindling joy, the silent prayer, would be dead to him. And he who, from a like physical point of view, gazes on the face of this universe, who presents himself before it as a foreigner with no sympathies to aid him, will find it all made up of matter and motion; he sees one thing standing beside another, and one change coming after another, but it will be the expression of no mind. Its space and silence will not look at him like the clearness of an everlasting brow. No awful Pity will watch him beneath the arch of night. No solemn Will flows down upon the streams; and the spring grass and the autumn forest will be simply a painted green and red without being felt as the blush of Thought coming to the surface. *Natural faith* is the essential root of all knowledge, love, and peace; whose place, do what you will, is not at the end, but at the beginning of thought; which gives to the intellectual faculties their only ground, instead of being indebted to them for its own; which, while allied with them, exchanges with them refinement and elevation, and forms a glorious nature; but, when divorced from them, dooms them and itself to dwindle and die. By *natural faith* I mean the assumption *that a Divine Perfection is the everlasting basis of all things*, that infinite Thought and Holiness are and ever must be at the helm of affairs, and that the universe is but the phenomenon for expressing God's eternal reality.

Apart from this faith, knowledge itself becomes lowered in its spirit and restricted in its blessing. Knowledge bears a double fruit —a physical and a moral. It enables us to *do more,* and disposes us to *be better.* But it is not the same kind of knowledge that effects both of these results. We increase our power by knowing objects that are beneath us; our goodness by knowing those that are above us. All the triumphs of the modern arts have been won by detecting the secret of some force inferior in quality to our own— some force, therefore, which we could transcend and subject to our convenience. Thus human thought has proved too much for the elasticity of steam, and sends it, like a captured bondsman, to do its task-work on the roads and in the ships. Electricity has been caught, despite its invisible wing, and made to fly to and fro on messages it knows not. Light has been trained to record and fix the images it creates, and paint portraits of the objects it reveals. In all such instances of new skill and enlarged resources, the advances of knowledge have been upon the physical laws of Nature; some conquered province of creation lies at our feet, and pays a tribute to our superiority. But who can say that we are *personally nobler* for this homage? The telegraph carries no redeeming shock to any guilty will; the sunbeam enables no deluded soul to see itself. Quicker voyages, more abundant jewelry, larger surfaces of silver, and unlimited square feet of glass, will not make one temper sweeter, or open a transparent way through the heart of selfishness and guile. An Eiffel tower, from its sublime height, may tell a story of stooping very low. If you could bridge the Atlantic, it would give a path to knaves as well as to honest men; and did you roof the world with crystal, it would make a winter garden for weeds as well as flowers. It is a fatal delusion to imagine that the arts of life, which only enlarge its resources, have any necessary tendency to improve its spirit; or that the completest acquaintance with science affords any guarantee of higher goodness. No laboratory can neutralise the poison of the passions, or find a crucible to make the hard nucleus of the heart flown down; no observatory can show us a new constellation of the virtues, correct the aberration of life's true light, or deepen any heavens but those of space. Scientific culture is morally neutral, simply enlarging the range without altering the quality of the character. If love and faith be brought into it, they will find the universe diviner than they had thought, and yet, with an elastic incense of contemplation, be able to fill it all with glory. If only the sharpness of sense and intellect be brought into it, nothing else will be fetched out of it, and where evil passions reign, new knowledge is as likely to become the implement of more powerful wickedness, as the limb which you restore for the crippled criminal, or the tool invented in a career of theft. The only knowledge that can really make us better is not of *things* and their laws, but of *persons* and their thoughts; and I would rather have an hour's sympathy with one noble heart than read the law of gravitation through and through. To teach us what to love and what to hate, whom to honour and whom to despise, is the substance of all human training, and this is not to be learned from the magnet or the microscope, from insects born in galvanism and light polarised in crystals, but only among the affairs of men; from the rich records of the past, the strife of heroic and the peace of saintly souls, from the great thoughts of great minds, and the sublime acts of indomitable conscience. The soul takes its complexion and its true port from the society in which it dwells; it lives with the living and dies with the dead, and no intimacy with rocks and reptiles, however enlarging to its conception of the world, can lift it to its dignity, and warm it with its proper glow; but only communion with the prophets, the patriot, the sage, the martyrs of the cross. It is the grand fault of our modern education—a fault which reaches its acme in the theory of a purely *secular* education—that we limit it to the mere knowledge of *things,* and, except where the Christian Scriptures save us from such blight, bring the scholar's mind into scarce any admiring contact with pre-eminent *persons.* We teach him the grammar and the forms of speech, but few of the things most worthy to be spoken. We teach him the seas and lands, the rivers and mountains of a dead or empty world, but of the histories they have passed there, the proud passages of his country's life, the good men that should be as the beacon to his path, we too often leave him in ignorance. We lost the true notion of human culture when we threw away the "*lives of the saints.*" The type of excellence which they held up was not, indeed, the right one, or worthy to be preserved in the place it claimed; but until they be rewritten with a better selection of examples, and be made the manual and favourites of the cottage and the school, all our education will multiply the force without greatly mending the character of our society. The soul grows godlike, not by its downward gaze at inferior nature, but by its uplifted look at thought and goodness greater than its own. Where there is *no faith*, where even *persons* are regarded as *things*—organisms moulded by the elements and galvanised across the stage—this attitude ceases to be possible; inferior nature becomes all in all, is itself the expression of no Thought, but the raw material of its manufacture, evolves every higher product out of the lower, so that the source of everything is the lowest of all, and the student's own genius and intelligence blindly issue from forces that neither live nor understand. Where the object known is not of higher nature than the knower, he contemplates it with *reverence* no more. He looks on material law as at once his creator and his slave, and the effect says to the cause, "*I* am the greatest thing that you have done; in making me you have made your master, who will turn you to unexpected account." In this mood knowledge is pushed forward only in the love of power, the passion for it sinks from a devoutness to an ambition, is no longer as the light upon a holy face, but as a flame upon the restless brow of demons, and seizes its desire like the mad draught of fever rather than as the solemn wine that has but to kiss the lips to become a sacrament. Nothing is so delirious, nothing so credulous, as this eagerness for *knowledge as power*, where the wisdom of faith is not present to restrain. Wild dreams of success, prophecies of magic triumphs, occupy and intoxicate the understanding; create impatience at the present, and throw contempt upon the past; impair the clearness of reason and observation; and entail all the delusions of a scornful mind. Modesty and humility are but expressions of a secret worship in the heart; they are that natural homage to the higher which cannot long subsist but in the overshadowing presence of the Highest of all. Apart from God we lose all our proportions; like the stones of the arch without their key, know not our place, but scramble into a level equality of ruin. And whoever sees the unloveliness of egotism and arrogance, and shrinks from the danger of them, must press close upon Him who holds us together, giving a use to each and a form of beauty to us all. He who ceases to kneel before the Divine wisdom, soon talks superciliously of the human, and ends with the worship of his own.

But, perhaps, in thus emphasizing *Faith*, I am disarranging the Christian graces, the supreme of which, I may be reminded, is neither "Faith," nor "Hope," but "*Love*." Yes; "Love is greatest" precisely because, in its Christian sense, it *presupposes* Faith and Hope, and is their working development and crown and, without them, remains a mere pathetic fondness, hardly deserving its name. How wide is the interval which separates its rudiments from its perfect type! If you love your *dog*, it is that you sympathise with his pleasures and pains, and reciprocate his attachment, and feel for his limitations, wishing that he could speak and tell all that his dumb looks imply. But the relation stops short with the present facts of a common animal nature; it has no future in it; it ends where the essence of your life begins. When you love your *child*, these rudiments are also there. But, as he leaps into your arms, you embrace him, less for what he *is* than for what he *is to be*. Besides *his* joy, which "comes first, as the natural," is *yours*, which transcends it, as "spiritual." You see in him a casket of immortal powers, whose guardian you are to be under the eye of God. Whatever this affection has beyond mere instinct is due to faith and hope, through which it blends the loveliest features of incipient finite nature with the glory of a spiritual infinitude. Again, perhaps you love some wise and saintly *friend*, the high level and tender beauty of whose life have made your own ill-ordered ways intolerable to you, and have led you through the discipline of service to the peace of God. What, then, is your devotion to him but the confluent flames of the faith which he has kindled, and the hope which he has justified? Or, once more, have you, with Christ-like pity, set your heart upon some soul desolate in guilt, which yields before your watchful eye and that alone, and so forbids you to go away, lest the wanderings return? Even here, what is the secret spring of that patient love but faith in the recuperative power of sustained repentance, and hope that beneath the quickening breath of a pure experience the spirit may yet be born again? *All* distinctively human love carries in it the vision of higher possibilities, so that its very essence is tinctured with *Reverence*—reverence for what is *promised* in the child; for what is *present* in the saint; for what is contingent, but *attainable*, in the sinner. And Reverence has no entrance except where souls are free, and not foredoomed to the better or the worse. Nor would God Himself be righteously adorable if His perfection were but an infinite Necessity. Vain and cruel would it *then* be to bid us be " perfect, as our Father in heaven is perfect "; and the declaration that "His thoughts are not as our thoughts" would have an absolute meaning more terrible than we could bear. Without the assurance, natural to a good heart, that intending thought and preferential holiness are the everlasting basis of the universe, intellect ceases to understand, and conscience bears false witness.

Every sympathetic observer of life must have noticed how the enthusiasm of Reverence declines with the fading away of Faith and Hope. In the mind which ceases to commune with the Supreme Perfection, the discernment of human excellence gradually loses its quickness; the feeling for it becomes changed and lowered; it is regarded with less of simple trust, with nothing of intent aspiration. It stands no longer upon "the hills whence cometh our help," and up which we press with eager feet and panting breast; but settles upon the flats of life, where we all herd together as boon companions of an earthly bounty. It is looked upon neither as the beauty of a heavenly grace, nor as the trophy of a faithful will; but, like a handsome figure or a fine complexion, as a happy combination of nature, *wholesome*, not holy. The world and its history, its muster-roll of consecrated names, its ranks of the brave and good, pass before such an eye like troops in a review; whose general, seeing a regiment of men six feet high and in the prime of life, says, "Fine fellows these!" The purest elements of affection are incompatible with this temper; did men live by its theory, they would have to choose a friend as they would buy a horse, looking at his points and showing off his paces. Where moral qualities are degraded to the level of natural, and treated as the product of material necessity, the well-springs of sacred love are quite dried up. When I love another, it is not because he ranges at the top of the Mammalia, but because his foot is on the steps of the ascent to God. If this be an optical delusion; if, when we look up together to higher altitudes, our hearts burn within us in vain; if, when I am weak and he is strong, I may not cling to him and bid him lift me by the virtue that goes out of the very hem of his garments; if the pyramid of souls up which we press has no summit in the heaven, but the attraction by which we climb on the one side is to become a depression for returning to the sands upon the other—then is all the nobleness of affection but the witchery of a lying spirit, and its elevation and tenderness exist no more. Whatever remits the tension of aspiration relaxes the embrace of love. The dear ties which weave our spirits into relations of interdependence are not the palpable things they seem to be, but twine around us as a mystic secret beneath the outer folds of life; and assuredly the tissue of mutual reverence that binds us to each other is the same that holds us all to God. Prospective faith alone supports the dignity and hopefulness of human affections. Without it there may indeed be abundance of good-humoured sympathy and indulgent pity; for moral repugnances having no ground left, all evil appears as a physical helplessness, and the range of compassion is so widened as to absorb into its channel all the currents of a good heart. It avails, no doubt, where thus enlarged, to quell the heats of anger, for what we pity we certainly cannot *hate;* but neither can we *honour* it; and the great problem of morals—how we are to keep the precept, "Honour all men," yet see all the meanness of many—is one which only Christian faith can solve. Living in mental contact with Infinite Holiness, the pure-minded man could never honour the guilty and degraded on their own account, and might be supposed to acquire, in the society of congenial spirits, an utter distaste for the lower throng of sinful beings. But there has been divinely shown to him a tree which, flung into the bitter waters, makes them sweet. Let him turn, in his thought of the wicked, from what they *are* to what they *might be*, and the turbid film of disgust will clear away from his heart, broken up and dispersed by lights of glorious capacity gleaming through the cloud of their ignorance and guilt. Knowing that the Divine affinity of spirit with spirit "is not dead within them, but only sleepeth," he looks on them with the prophetic eye of trust; and without the least reconcilement (indeed, with less than ever) to what they now are, he is touched with anticipatory reverence for what they are meant to be. He alone who thus lives as seeing the invisible, can face the saddest human realities, yet lose no reverential affection. He loves imperfect beings as a mother loves her wayward child, and kisses away its passion and its tears; bearing with all their weaknesses for God's sake, who has set them at the parting of the broad and narrow ways as the needful discipline of freedom, and the alternative of all holy possibility. Nay, once possessed by this faith, he not only *reads* the Divine possibilities, but *starts and evolves* them, by assuming them in other souls, and waking them into living power by the thrilling truth of his appeal. From such a One it is that even enemies turn back with the words "Never man spake like this Man"; and wherever his Spirit repeats itself in His disciples, you will not look in vain for "the dead that are alive again, and the lost that are found."

The Lapse of Time, and the Law of Obligation.

THE LAPSE OF TIME, AND THE LAW OF OBLIGATION.

"While the earth remaineth, seed-time and harvest, and cold and heat, and summer and winter, and day and night, shall not cease."—GENESIS viii. 22.

WHOEVER may step out into his garden or throw up his window, to breathe the first air of a new day or a new year, cannot fail to be struck with the insensibility of nature to our divisions of time. The greater and the lesser lights of the sky feel not the seasons of which they are appointed to be signs. No great bell of the universe tolls away the passing spirit of the year; no chimes ring out from the restless wind to greet the period new-born. The calm, eternal heavens maintain their silent steadfastness, the star slips past the meridian wire which divides century from century, as though it were a vulgar moment, without pause to think or trembling to feel how awful the mark it sets afloat on the current of eternity. The unconscious earth lies still and patient as before, feeling only how the trees rooted in its bosom are leaning and rocking in the night breeze, and its snow-mantle is folded here and unfolded there with caprices stranger than a child's. No stream suspends its song to listen to the moments flowing by, no tide stands still to watch that wondrous sea of time that ever ebbs, yet never fails. Even life in its several forms and generations exhibits the same passionless continuity, and glides from era to era without a celebration. The cautious bud skulks near the bark, and sleeps unmoved within its varnished case, watching the royal sun as its thermometer, but heedless of him as its timepiece. The animals browse on or sleep through crises the most impressive. And the men whose life goes by the pulsations of their blood, rather than the colours of their thought, to whom, sensation remaining the same, nothing becomes materially different, have no days in their calendar chalked with the white mark of sanctity; but remember their anniversaries mainly by their dinners, and would lie down at the most solemn point of history, if it happened to be time to rest.

At the instant when lower nature exhibits this unconscious uniformity, many a wakeful mind recognises a transition of the deepest import. Though the bridge which stretches from year to year exists only in our idea, it is a station most real and most commanding. The perspective of the past, with its sharp forms, its clear light, its receding groups, its boundary circle of protecting hills, lies open to the eye of love; and the hazy passes of the future, with only gleams of glorious sunshine cutting across the deepest darkness, and facing the mountain shades with the green-painted slope, invite the heart of mystery. How plain, as we stand there, becomes the sense of what we are and what we were! With how brilliant a sadness do the young hopes, the high resolves, the capacious ambitions of our fresh days, revisit our humbled hearts! As we look into the midnight of the departing year, how do the radiant images of blessings lost glow amid the space, till, as they begin to smile on us again, the darkness closes round them, and the saintly sight is gone! And even when we call around us the living company of friends, the most cheerful eye cannot wander over the circle without many a pause of serious wonder. The recent child that has the stature of the man; the infant we have nursed that is now the mother; the fresh, careless youth faded perhaps into morose, disappointed manhood, and sunk from a fair promise into a false prime; the comely form of many a matron, faint and drooping now; the brow no longer smooth, the hand no longer firm; the lines of sorrow on the cheek, deeper than the tracery of age; and all the hieroglyphics of mortality,—make us feel that we do not share the immobility, and cannot affect the indifference, of mechanical nature; and convince us, as we hear the great wheel of Necessity humming its dreadful monotony, that we must either rise into a transcendent faith, or fall into a sad despair. Whoever is imbued with the wisdom of a pure heart, and touched with the simplicity of Christ, will check the rush of feeling towards confusion; and surveying the field of life from the high station of love and faith, remain to the end master of its priceless opportunities.

The habit of regarding time rather as a physical than as a human thing is connected with not a little low morality, and dictates many a sentimental thought, whose currency ought not to hide from us its falsehood. It is often said that the lapse of years affects our duty by shortening the period of service; that the nearer we are brought to the limit of our present career, the more does it behove us to make haste and overtake our work; that the lessening sum of moments must be spent in making ready for our change of scene. And if this be meant only as a suggesof natural feeling, or compunction for past remissness, it states what will approve itself to every good mind. It is not fit for man to walk blindly to such a migration as death; so great a thing can be worthily approached only with the open eye of reason and of trust; and whoever knows that it is not far, as the martyr waiting for the kindling of his fires, or as the aged and stricken, whose summons has been signed and whose respite cannot be prolonged, will fall into a corresponding attitude of thought and find some soft and solemn hues steal over his affections. He cannot but stand upon the watch ready for the hint that trembles on the confines of the hour, for it is not in our nature to feel no difference between a near certainty and a far; and when, by altered place, the distance has become the foreground, it would argue an unmanly insensibility did it not engage us more. But this is simply the natural posture of the affections in an unperverted mind; it is not a matter of obligation. It expresses preparation, but does not constitute it; it reveals the Christian lineaments, but does not trace them. Much more than this is implied in the usual lessons drawn from the lapse of years; and it greatly concerns our primary notions of Christian duty to understand the precise manner in which that duty is affected by the seasonal changes of our life.

Strictly speaking, very little in relation to man's duty depends on the diminishing quantity of his time to come. Whether it be a day or a half-century makes no difference in the nature or the intensity of his moral obligation, though it must doubtless affect the external actions on which it may be rational for him to enter. Nay, if there were no such thing as death for him at all; if he had the early Christian's expectation of immortality on earth; the sentence of reprieve for his animal nature would bring no release from the glorious bonds that are laid upon the spiritual. Every hour would retain its priceless worth, notwithstanding the most copious supply; nor could eternity itself cheapen the moments entrusted to his will. When Paul gained the conviction that he was raised above the touch of mortality; when he first looked into the opening avenue of ages and saw himself, with living feet, securely passing through; when he felt that he could defy the perils of shipwreck and the sword of persecution, did it abate his earnestness, and whisper to him that he had time enough? Did it turn his eager haste into an easy stroll? Did it fill him with moral indifference to the world that slumbered above the elements of explosion? Far otherwise. It cooled his personal interests, and made him so far of quiet heart; but it set his conscience on fire, and he spake the truth, he soothed the sorrows, he warned the sins, which would have been the objects of his care had he beheld that age of Providence as we look back upon it now. "What would you wish to be doing," was the question once put to a wise man, "if you knew that you were to die the next minute?" "Just what I am doing now," was his reply, though he was neither repeating the creed, nor telling his religious experience; but, for aught I know, posting his accounts, or talking merry nonsense with his children round the fire. Nothing that is worthy of a living man can be unworthy of a dying one; and whatever is shocking in the last moment would be disgraceful in every other. The most trivial things, in their order and season, lose their moral incongruity and meanness; the most lofty, when misplaced, are deprived of all their greatness. He who is snatched from the world at his prayers when his work is overdue may well pass with culprit heart away; while the punctual Christian need not be scared to find himself brushing his hat within a minute's reach of the saints in heaven. In truth, it is impossible to borrow motives from the mere approach of death without withdrawing them from the other parts of life. If, as our term hastens to expire, we have just reason for putting forth *more strenuous* service, then, in proportion to the remoteness of the goal, we must have reason equally just for *less strenuous* service ; our obligations must present a series of quantities in increasing ratio; there must be times unruled or slightly touched by Conscience when its authority is inchoate and immature. Were it thus, sins of deepest dye in a life that had a year to run would have a lighter shade if five remained, and might be all together bleached by exposure to twenty summer suns. I need not say how degrading it is thus to assign chronology to the rule of duty, to give shifting seasons to immutable Law. It is to look at the most solemn of realities through illusions of our fancy, to suppose the holiness of God capable of relaxation and intensity by changes purely physical, to subject His approval to our laws of mental distance. The proximity of death may, indeed, open our eyes, and startle us with the consciousness of truths but ill-discerned before, but the truth itself was no less there; the duty so pressing on our hand is not created, but only found; the neglect that weighs newly on the heart is not a product of to-day, but oh, of how wearisome an age!

Thus there is always a lax side to this sort of morality. It connives at our waiting to be faithful till we can scarcely help it, and by pressing us to future haste slurs over past delay. If it be possible thus to make up for lost time, then human duty must be a kind of task-work, assigned in definite quantity to our hand, with no stipulation but that at some time or other it shall be done. If it be capable of compression it must admit of dilution; remissness may be compensated by diligence, and early assiduity may exhaust and prematurely finish up our obligations. Against a conception so base every true soul presents an involuntary remonstrance. This responsible existence is not a gaol, in which we are imprisoned on the ticket system, and permitted to work out our term of hard labour, and by good use of spare hours go free into idleness and ease for ever after. Its sacred bondage is no state of miserable punishment, of grievous expiation, to be sighed over and gone through, but of severe and glorious privilege, which once embraced can never be resigned; to be clung to through the changes of death as of life, like the piercing yet saving crucifix of self-denial. It is as the vow of pilgrimage to a holy land, the sepulchre of saviours and of saints, the field of prophets' glory, the mount of Divine transfiguration, which, real as it is in God's universe, lies nowhere in our geography; to which we take our passage in vain by any steamship; which the Bishop of Jerusalem cannot help us to find out; the very light of whose beauty and colours of whose identity appear to have fled, as we stand upon the common hills and look into the turbid streams, yet whose image, ineffaceable from our believing hearts, still tempts us on, explorers of successive worlds, and devoted to an endless quest. Whoever cannot resign himself to an absolute impossibility of moral collapse and rest, however much he may have achieved—whoever wishes to earn his discharge from the service of God by the length of his fidelity, is a stranger yet to the true and loyal heart, and has taken the vow of the hireling, not the sacrament of love. On this,

THE LAW OF OBLIGATION. 55

indeed, rests all the talk about its being time to prepare for the change of worlds. It implies that our duty is but a means to a future end, the medicine followed by the sweetmeats; that the period of our submission to it is soon to close; that we shall then have done with it, and reached the great holiday of our existence. This is to renounce the primary sentiments of conscience, to refuse the authority of God. It denies His Divine right over us, and sets Him on the level, bargaining with us. It abrogates the whole law of obligation; proclaims that there is nothing above interest; establishes the worship of wages; and degrades heaven and immortality into a gigantic pay-day. I know of no more shameful profanation of great and holy realities. The doctrine of retribution is most true and solemn, but it constitutes no duty; it changes none; it implies them all. If we were not bound without it, we should still be free to please ourselves under it; and it would be nobody's affair but ours if we chose to pocket our remorse and take the consequences. No, it is not retribution that establishes the moral law, but the moral law that establishes retribution. The shadow falls not *backward* from that world to this, but *forward* from this world to that. It is our nature and our conscience that demand and must determine our future lot; not our future lot that is to create our conscience and regulate our nature. The true disciple's heart claims no recompense, but renders willing service after service, "hoping for nothing again"; and though full of high expectancy, and lighted with the immortal glow, deriving thence nothing of the faithfulness of duty, but only its grandeur and its joy; content to be among the "children of the Highest," whether in one world or in two, for an hour or for untold years.

While nothing, in relation to human duty, depends on the *diminishing quantity of our time to come*, everything depends on the *ever-changing quality of present objects and events;* and thus it is that the lapse of years reads the true lesson to our conscience. The mere flight of dead and empty duration, and our own particular relation to it, are of little moment; but the shifting attitudes of the things within it, the vicissitudes of the beings it contains, are of the highest and most fearful concern. They are the conditions of all our action, whose happy adaptation to them constitutes our moral wisdom; whose disregard of them makes our negligence; whose variance from them creates our folly and our sin. We live in a world of progress and unrest. Every object by which we are surrounded is passing through evanescent states, which must be caught or they are gone; and since all our work, not being a mere flourish of activity in emptiness, has constant reference to these, there is not a particle of it that can wait. If it is not struck down upon the instant its solid efficiency is all wasted, and its movement only beats the air. It is not the seasons only and the clouds that change from day to day; so that if you cut not your corn by the timely autumn sun, the hail will pelt out and the damp skies rot the hopes of the year. But there is nothing that stands still in time, so that no duty at all admits of delay; each is strictly the duty of the moment; and our moral life is a race of perpetual speed, in which, at every step, the ground breaks from beneath us, and if our foot be not ready for the advance we must sink with it and fall away. The child, neglected to-day, is less teachable tomorrow; his pliant and submissive heart, permitted to collect the crust of ignorant self-will, will need some softening ere you can begin; and his eager questions, betraying the wide-open mind, once pushed rudely back, you cannot gain entrance till by false keys you have unclosed the curiosity that was suffered to collapse. The act of social kindness, which is a gracious attention this week, becomes an overdue debt the next, and is presented with sad apology instead of received with glad surprise. The want which we vainly purposed to relieve soon looks up at us with reproachful face from the still graves. The tears we failed to wipe away dry upon the cheek, and leave us in the presence of the averted features of distrust instead of the eye of sweet reliance. The wounded tenderness to which we spoke not the timely and soothing word, passes into permanent soreness, instead of healing into grateful love. All round our human existence, indeed, does this same thing appear. The just expectation which we have disappointed cannot be recovered; there must be a long undoing before you can weave again, in even lines and pattern fair, the tangled web of life. Simply to reinstate the former conditions that should never have become confused is ever a vast and weary task; a barren and negative necessity, fruitless of positive good, the mere burdensome creation of our negligence. It is truly humiliating to think how enormous a proportion of the world's activity is spent upon the mere repair of evils occasioned by human unfaithfulness. When the physician has reckoned all the diseases and sufferings be witnesses which involve any element of guilt; when the lawyer has counted the suits brought to him by fraud, injustice, and cupidity; when the tradesman has told how much of the cost he incurs is in looking up the debts which else would not be paid, or watching the servants who cannot be trusted out of sight; when the labour has been weighed, which is occasioned wholly by broken promises, and disappointed expectations, and interrupted contracts, how much, think you, would remain to constitute the real productive and progressive work of mankind, compensative of no artificial evil, but fulfilling the appointed Providential good? If every posture of things were seized by the faithful conscience at the right moment, and no crisis were lost, who will venture to say what sorrows would be saved, what complications would be unravelled, or even what interval would be left between the heaven we hope for and the earth we live in? Nor must we forget that while objects around us perpetually change we ourselves do not stand still. We also are subjects of transient and evanescent states, bringing with them their several obligations, and carrying away their fruits of tranquility or of reproach. Each present conviction, each secret suggestion of duty, constitutes a distinct and separate call of God, which can never be slighted without the certainty of its total departure or its fainter return. The spontaneous movement of the heart can then only be replaced by the strivings of a heavy and reluctant Will, with twice the work and only half the strength. The different feeling of to-morrow is destined to a different work, and cannot be diverted to accomplish the task which was due to-day. And so the power which is not wisely spent must be wildly wasted. Our true opportunities come but once; they are sufficient but not redundant; we have time enough for the longest duty, but not for the shortest sin.

Thou Art My Strength.

THOU ART MY STRENGTH.

"I can of mine own self do nothing."—
JOHN v. 30.

WHAT is the *"own self"* between which and *"the Father"* in heaven Jesus, in thus speaking, marks the distinction? Where is the line intended to be drawn which parts the two agencies, and what are the works characteristic of each? Must we place on the one side the familiar stock of powers constituting the human kind, and conducting the routine of common life, and on the other the exceptional intervention of the Supreme Will declaring itself in signs and wonders?

To take it thus would be to narrow grievously the scope of the thought. It is not miracle alone which Jesus ascribes to the Father dwelling in Him, while retaining all else for His own personality. It would be but a vapid tautology to say that His humanity was incompetent to the superhuman. No; the power which He disclaimed for Himself was, nevertheless, not foreign to Himself. It was in Him, yet not of Him; it came to Him, and yet was at home; it was from above Him, and yet " worked with Him to will and to do." Nay, it was an enthusiasm for "whatsoever things He saw the Father doing " in the hearts of men and the government of the world; a love of the deeper meanings hid, as the secret of God, beneath the surface of life, and yet, to the sympathetic eye, rendering it transparent with a light of beauty. On "the Father showing Him all things that Himself doeth," how else could the Son respond than by "doing just those things in like manner"? *That* was the presence in His soul, *that* the living touch of Divine Perfection, which lifted Him out of His "own self," and made Him the vehicle of a transcendent spirit of righteousness.

In this view the power here disclaimed by Jesus and referred to God is the same in kind with that which the Apostle Paul refers to Christ, when he says, "I can *do all things* through Christ that strengtheneth me." This was not the gift of miracle, not the implanting of knowledge exotic to the mind, not any superhuman attribute conferred by Jesus in personal visitations, but the simple might of spiritual self-devotion, imparted by *the idea of his great model* dwelling ever near his conscience; which taught him, with scarce the consciousness of effort, "both how to be abased and how to abound." It was the force derived from the tension of full affections, by which they crush resistance, and roll out the most massive difficulties into films that may be whiffed before the wind. It was the power natural to his grateful and loving mind, solely occupied as it was by the conception of One who had been that mind's emancipator, by delivering his worship from the bondage of ceremony, his understanding from the sophistry of persecution, and his heart from the miseries of contempt. From the thought of this holy and immortal Son of God there passed into his will a transforming energy, which, it was hardly an exaggeration to say, enabled him to "do all things." For against what defiances did he match himself in vain? Who at the end of life could look back on a career of such various resolve, of toils despised, of perils passed, of unforfeited constancy to truth, as lay beneath the retrospect of "Paul the Aged"? What veteran leader, pierced in the hour of victory, could hear, as he fell, a shout of exultation so cheering as the concurrent sympathies amid which Nero's sword dismissed the apostle to his rest? Alone he had thrown himself into the crowd of Gentile peoples, to whom, as a Hebrew of the Hebrews, he was an object of twofold scorn; and by the patience of his will ruling an impassioned heart and ennobling a fervid speech had won audience for the story of Christ from Arabia to Rome. He had made guilty power tremble on its seat at his voice, that seemed charged with the authority of Righteousness itself. On "Mars Hill" he had stood face to face with the gods of Athens, with the dread cave of the Eumenides beneath his feet, as he invoked

Jehovah, Lord of the heaven above him, to take possession of the heart of this living people, and claim the blue Ægean as his own. He maintained the toil of a mechanic that he might perform better the duty of an apostle. Persecuted from city to city, he forgot the foes behind and hoped for friends before. He is cast into prison; and he makes a Christian of the gaoler, and leaves him to preach to his captives ever after the glad tidings of great joy. He tranquilises the terrors of shipwreck by his counsel; and, guarded by a sentinel at Rome, he goes forth under cover of the darkness to seek the haunts of misery, and kneeling by the pallet of the sick slave breathe a prayer of strange refreshment, bringing to the suffering heart the protection of a fatherly God and the sympathy of a brother man. The threats against his life never damp the manhood of his spirit; but his fettered hand writes many a letter free and bold that bears his cheerful vigour through the churches, and sends a throb of nobler life through the infant heart of Christendom.

It was the image and the love of Christ that gave Paul this various power; and it was the vision, the love, the spiritual touch of God without which Christ could do nothing. Thus he explains his own meaning when, immediately after my text, he says that he "seeks not his own will, but the will of the Father who sent him"; and, just before, that "he can do *nothing, except what he sees the Father do.*" The thought of God within his conscience was his strength; and did he think of himself he would instantly sink in weakness. He lets us into the secret here—not of his physical power to work miracles, but of his spiritual power to transform the ideal of righteousness for the world. And in doing so he bears personal testimony to a profound and simple truth; that a mere prudential virtue, though extending its reckoning from earth to heaven, can attain no greatness; that the most refined considerations of interest are powerless in the grander emergencies of life, and are forgotten in all acts which are venerable and holy; that out of the idea of self there comes no miracle. Self-regarding motives are unable to initiate the highest acts and offices of duty; these must remain unperformed unless some great moral passion imparts the requisite energy. The sterner services which society has a right to expect from faithful hands—which at all times may imperil ease and reputation, and in evil days involve liberty and life—would never be undertaken on the most exhaustive computation of advantage to the agent. At such an instigation what tongue would ever plead for truth unpopular and dangerous?— dangerous, I mean, to the advocate himself; and unpopular, not with an absent multitude whom it is easy to disregard, but with his neighbours and his hearers, whose derision he witnesses, and whose alienation his loneliness forces him to feel? What arm would ever strike the first blow at a powerful wrong, and be uplifted in the vow of self-dedication, often that of self-immolation, to the redemption of the oppressed? Where, amid the prevalence of such a spirit, would the despised, the outcast, the slave, the guilty, find a friend to notice them beneath the eye of day? No; Providence, as if to break the crust of our selfishness, has decreed that for the best blessings of this world men must venture something, must often venture themselves. Progressive knowledge, liberty, religion, are not won without a thousand risks; pearls not to be had without a plunge. And those who do not think the moral relations of men perfect as they are, those who are possessed with the conception and desire of a new and happier world, where crushing want need not exist, and character may stand at a higher level, and Religion clear itself into sublimer power, must look for it across the margin of present darkness and threatening deeps; they must listen with no landman's shudder to the waves, but go forth in faith like Columbus of old, when, haunted by the vision of some happy isles, or continent of unknown wealth and brighter suns, he dashed into the Atlantic storms that had beat upon no sail before, and still, amid want and discontent, steered onward to the West, looking forth from his prow from midnight to dawn till the bird brought tidings that his prophecy was true, and he anchored in the green waters of his promised land. I care not to decide whether the spirit of moral enterprise in such cases is really an imprudence; let the Utilitarian make out, if he can, that it is justified by considerations of comprehensive self-interest; and that the sympathetic affections which it exercises are far richer in happiness than the physical and other advantages which it forfeits. But I do say that this is not the estimate which we shall make at the moment which calls for action; *then* the refined satisfactions of the conscience and the heart have no chance against the importunity of nearer and more measurable benefits. And even if they had— if a self-regarding judgment were passed in their favour, and we said, "Oh, we will make a sacrifice of our comforts for the sake of getting the pleasures of benevolence," they would be beyond our reach; for the affections refuse to be deliberately made the tools of prudence, and obstinately fly when sought in such a spirit. Let them alone, and they will do their duty; count on them and canvass them, and they withhold their aid. Even those who maintain that acts of high courage and noble virtue *may have* their birth in a wise prudence must acknowledge that this has not actually been their usual origin; that the great and excellent whose names humanity holds most dear have, *in fact,* left unused the motives of personal welfare by which they might have been determined in their choice, and have been impelled by some mighty passion of good into which the idea of self could not enter. In truth, our best affections have that in their very nature which prevents them from being objects of anticipation: when their power is not on us we know not what they are, and, in indolent and selfish conditions of the mind, they are like a life forgotten in the draughts of sin. They are, indeed, the very essence of that heaven which "it doth not enter into the heart of man to conceive." They ever surprise us with their blessedness; we expect a stranger, and find an angel as our guest. The prevailing idea of Self introduces a moral weakness into the will, even in cases where there seems to be no call for disinterestedness, and the duty required appears mainly prudential. The struggles against guilty habits are, I believe, often unsuccessful, so long as they are the mere struggles of self-interest. Many a victim of some wretched vice is warned of his delusion; hears the whole list of its results; sees distinctly the picture of his shattered life, trembling at every breath without, and gnawed by self-contempt within; weeps burning tears, and frames passionate resolves; and yet secretly feels as if the springs of sincerity were not touched, and the probe had not reached his volitions yet. He feels the contortions of misery, but not the stirrings of a better life; and the reaction of cheerfulness brings the madness back again, and once more the will lies prostrate in shame and agony. And thus might the alternation go on did not some one come to him with reasons perhaps not half as strong but more affectionate; turn away his thoughts from the loathsome image of himself; fix them on his children whom it is not too late to save, or his parents who may yet be comforted; call them to some enterprise of compassion that may claim the whole faculty of an intense nature; tell him how Jesus looked with a holy mercy upon guilt, and it broke into instant tears, and ask him to bend low his head before the Father divine, and breathe forth a tranquil confession of unfaithfulness, and then, with his image and spirit fresh taken to the heart, aspire meekly to a restored mind. There are probably few who have not occasionally met with instances of an apparently wayward recovery from a life long marked by profligate self-indulgence; where, after the repeated failure of all rational remonstrance, something which seems to us a whimsical fanaticism is taken up, and suddenly the libertine becomes a saint; and in spite of the world's vulgar insinuation of hypocrisy, and cruel predictions of relapse, the pure will keeps its ascendant seat, and, however weary in some moments of the race, drives the chariot of the passions in safety to the goal. The theory of these cases is far more honourable to them, I believe, than our distaste to everything unreasonable permits us to allow. They are cases of minds that out of the thought of self can do nothing; but press the lever of their affections, and though it seems to have nothing whereon to rest you will move their world.

And if the thought of self is

unable to exert the best power over our own minds, still more signally does it fail to give us power over others. A purely self-regarding being is necessarily a solitary being; his hand is with no man, and he can expect no man's hand to be with him. If he be wise, there may be those that use his counsel; if he be the possessor of genius, there may be those that like to see it shine; if he be rich, there will be those that court his favour; if he be the leader of a party, there will be numbers in his train; but one who is unlearned and poor and private, and yet rich in the endowments of the conscience and the heart, will exert a diviner and vaster energy. The planets that have most satellites careering round them are most in the dark themselves. To have dependents moving about our power is poor compensation for banishment from the central love; and the full grandeur of that gloomy world which, with its apparatus of rings and moons, rides so royally through the colder planetary tracks, is less fair than the merest crescent of the morning star, bathed in the intenser flood of solar light. The wills of men may, of course, be influenced by all who have fears and hopes at their command—who have anything either to give or take away; and minds with gigantic force of determination may produce, without much moral principle, or any benevolence, or exceptional reach of understanding, a deep impression upon society; chiefly, however, upon the yielding and unresisting mass, who do not preserve the same shape and pressure from age to age, and can give perpetuity to nothing. Those only who have penetrating sympathies and a devotion to something more permanent than mere conventionalism and expediency can cut deep into the few firm minds who preserve the traces of the past for the uses of the future. Compare any set of dealings with the human mind conducted with the presence and in the absence of the thought of self. In education what wonders are wrought by the teacher becoming in heart a child, and laying aside all his maturity except its wisdom! Instead of listless attention, and irritable tempers, and half-realised ideas, and incessant complaint of perplexity, and a hatred of all knowledge precisely in proportion to its value, he that can clothe himself with his infancy again sees around him every symptom of happy and successful instruction; the unlanguid eye, the eager voice, the delighted onslaught upon a difficulty, all the indescribable natural language of a mind alert, a conscience quick, and spirits pure and light. In literature, the productions thrown off as a bid for gain or fame have never enjoyed an influence comparable, in durability and extent, with the power won by the spontaneity of genius, and the fervid simplicity of conviction disinterestedly surrendered to free creation. Does any one suppose that a hireling pen could have indited Milton's immortal pleas for purity in the Church and just liberty of speech and action in the State? Or that the cynical exaggerations and stormy grandeur of Byron will endure and rule as long as the pure truth of Wordsworth — the growth, not of the hotbed of passion, but of the sunny slopes and forest walks of love and meditation? No; all that is most permanent in our intellectual wealth issues from the interior and disinterested realm of our nature. Only in the rarest souls, at best, are forces lodged adequate to produce lasting effects of good upon a world little penetrable by individual effort; and nothing less intense than the central fires of the heart can open clefts in the rocky structure of society, and project the precious metals of true sentiment through its mass; the convulsion, it may be, of one age, but the riches of all others.

The same truth is found to hold in every other department of human agency. In every effort at persuasion, how puny are the ingenuities of art compared with the majesty of simple conviction and earnest purpose! In every attempt at social reformation, the power which begins with selfish expediency goes over in the end to the faithful few who refuse to cure one wrong by recourse to another. The assertion is not true, which we often hear, that the most remarkable triumphs won by decision of character are to be found among the bad; the most numerous successes may be theirs, but by far the grandest prodigies of human volition are recorded of the champions of the right; with the magnitude of whose achievements even in the field not the love of glory itself can contend. We are often deceived by the length of time required to ripen the successes of conscience. Jesus said, "I have come in My Father's name, and ye receive Me not; if another shall come in his own name, him ye will receive." And so, doubtless, it would have been; and that other would perchance have gathered no "*little flock*," like that to whom it was the Father's good pleasure to give the kingdom; he might have heard the acclamations of greater multitudes than cried on behalf of Jesus, "Hosanna to the Son of David"; he might have found a throne instead of a sepulchre among his people; and then would have perished as a rebel against Rome, instead of rising to be the moral Saviour of the world. The very nation on whose fortunes such a pretender would have based his ambition is swept away; its glory is a tradition and a dream; the place that once knew it shall know it no more. Meanwhile, the tale of the man of Nazareth lives and spreads, perforating with its sweet melodies the shout of battles and the storm of time; refreshing still the heart of poverty and the downcast penitence of sin; floating over the mutable tide of civilisation as it passes from shore to shore; and bearing faithful spirits to His own abode of rest. Such are the triumphs and immortality of conscience and inward truth. But self is a feeble and a barren thing, and out of it such wonder will never come.

The Claims of Christian Enterprise.

THE CLAIMS OF CHRISTIAN ENTERPRISE.

"In lowliness of mind let each esteem other better than themselves. Look not every man on his own things, but every man also on the things of others."—PHILIPP. ii. 3, 4.

IF we cast our eye over the names held by us in the most honourable remembrance, we find them invariably belonging to men who have quitted the common path of human duty, and gone out after disinterested ends foreign to their private sphere. Even the fruitless austerities of the ascetic, however exposed to the scorn of reason, are not without a sincere charm for the imagination; for they attest at least a self-dedication to the idea of Divine perfection, a preference of goodness to ease, so powerful as to carry the will beyond the requirements on which men insist. They seem to show a generous and ungrudging spirit that is not content with paying the tax of effort imposed by the moral law, but freely throws into the service of duty a spontaneity of sacrifice demonstrative of a faithfulness beyond all bondage. When Francis Xavier exchanges the inheritance of wealth and the pursuits of philosophy for the vows of poverty and exile, transferring his genius and energy from Europe, where they might have ranked in the van of civilisation, to the obscure East, where they could only serve in the rear of barbarism, and assumes the garb of pilgrim or of prince, if he may but lift the cross to nations unapproachable before, our hearts confess the justice with which he is numbered with the saints, and scarcely blame the superstition which says there is a sweet fragrance in the sands of China consecrated by his remains. Oberlin, quitting the society of equals and the presence of every refined sympathy, to spend his substance and his life in planting the Christian culture among the neglected mountaineers of Vosges; Clarkson, smitten to the heart by the spectacle of an unendurable iniquity, and living only for its abatement; Elizabeth Fry, snatched from vanities without and vanities within by her sweet faith in the all-conquering power of Divine truth and love, her assurance that prison walls and iron bars are no hindrance to the Holy Spirit, and that where God's whisper of recall finds it not too mean to go, her voice need not be ashamed to speak the open word: these, with all the noble host of heaven's missionaries and martyrs, kindle in us all a passionate homage, and fill us with a respect for our nature, and a new hope for the world. The biographies of such persons form an unacknowledged, yet a real, portion of the Bible of our hearts, and the sacred Canon of our life; nor has

Christ Himself any higher office than to concentrate upon Himself all the scattered lights of their separate excellence, and become the effulgent centre of that trust and reverence which they distribute over history. He was the culminating instance of goodness that did not remain at home; of patience not satisfied with its own sorrows; of sanctity which at once garrisoned the citadel of His individual mind, and involuntarily sought an empire in the soul of the world; of positive and aggressive devotedness that could not dwell in a village, or serve only an age, but "went about doing good," wherever grief and sin invited Him; first, of His own will, from city to city of His native province; and then of God's will, from land to land, and from age to age of human history. What is it that so subdues us in these souls of large adventure, and makes us gather round them as the very saviours of our faith, compelling us to feel that, were their names not there, the record of mankind would be a dreary thing, and were their voices silent, the course of time would have no music in its flow? Surely it is no sense of selfish benefit, no grateful thought of what they may have gained for us. We measure them, not by their success, but by their worth; and had their striving been in vain we should have loved them still, only with a sadness instead of a glory in the heart.

No; they wield over us the double power of rebuke and prophecy; they show us our aspirations realised, and tell us that our conscience does not dream; their self-denials put our comforts to the blush; their heavenly constancy looks down, as from a clearer region, upon the fickle clouds of our inferior mind; we long to escape from our tangled plausibilities to their pure simplicity, and from our fretful fears to their trustful courage. They reveal to us the spirit of the life we ought to live, and present us to the God who will uphold us in it. In our admiration of the nobly good there is always a tacit reference to our own unsatisfying state, a secret weeping of the soul over its meanness and its misery, and a gleam of freshening hope like the first spring day to the invalid. Thus, it is as eternal oracles and interpreters of conscience that it is given to the " saints to judge the world."

" Yet are we required," the sober critic may ask, " to live as they ? Was their course even one that can be wisely approved ? While they are away nursing the stranger in the infirmary of human ills, may not the sickness, in this plague-stricken world, have broken out at home ? Surely it can never be meant that we should leave our own sphere to be cared for by others, while we are spending our zeal on theirs ? Were all to turn out under vows of ascetic sacrifice or missionary devotion, life could not go on; the depository of intensest energy, all its force would be ineffectual; just as the fastest atmosphere, meeting no resistance but flying as a whole, is virtually at rest and may carry within it the malaria of stagnation. The work, moreover, which has engaged the hand of saintly men is no legitimate task of Providential creation —no pity for natural ills—but is the artificial product of human wickedness, the redress of injustice, the repair of guilty neglect; and is it not a premium on the world's unfaithfulness to take the bitter ashes of death out of its mouth, and, unasked, give it in instead the healing fruit of life? Under a holy God can the penalties of sin and the performance of duty be allowed to become vicarious, so that I am to be my brother's keeper? Must not rather every man bear his own burden? Did each in his time and place punctually occupy his own succession of obligations; did he suppress every rising desire in his heart and in his home; did he break no resolve, forget no promise, sleep through no crisis of opportunity — the very ills that challenge our heroes to the conflict would never arise: the fidelity of each would create a Paradise for all; or, at least, only light and tranquil sorrows would remain. If the earth exhibits darker shades, this is chargeable, not on good punctual souls who pay the debts of conscience as they are due, but to spendthrift and insolvent sinners, who reduce the accounts with heaven to bankruptcy. What more, then," it may be said, "can be asked of me than that I do my personal share towards the order and peace and virtue of the world? I tell no lies, steal no man's goods, break no trust; my children are taught, my servants well treated, my friends not forgot; no slander defiles my lips, no suspicion darkens my thought; appetite is under temperate rule, and no time is given to sloth and vanity. If all men would do the same, how little would there be to desire! Evil being prevented, there would be scarce any good to do."

Thus are we driven in opposite

directions of feeling respecting the heroes of the cross: impelled to enlist under them, and to desert from them; brought to their feet by natural reverence, and then by a theory of common-sense withdrawn in shame at our enthusiasm. But let us not hastily discard the first persuasion, or trust ourselves to the narrower interpretation of God's will; perhaps the truth of both may be reconciled, or the falsity of one detected. Certain it is, and a *suspicious* certainty, that the view which looks so rational is pleaded for by all that is poor and low in us, and delivers us from the noblest and most productive sorrows of the soul. All the lazy conservatism of self-righteous habit is on its side.

There are men, and there are moods in all men, that cannot bear to be reproached, and that feel hurt by only the silent presence of a humiliating goodness; that, by infusion of a poisonous self-love, have degraded conscience to a mere sensitive and vulnerable complacency; and at the first touch of aspiration, catch the disease of envy. To such minds this easy little theory, that duty begins at home, insidiously appeals; it takes off the sense of insignificance, relieves the burden of repentance, and administers the consolations of calumny. "Those self-denying people resist their appetites," we say, "that they may better pamper their spiritual pride; and the private households of your roving philanthropists would seldom bear," we insinuate, "any strict examination; so that, after all, they only abandon a duty on which no eye is fixed for one which brings a consecrated applause." Oh! it is a dangerous and beguiling thing to sit thus in conjectural judgment on what we have felt to be above us; to exchange the bowed head and hidden face of reverence for the bold front and petulant glance of the critic and the objector; to repent of our purest admirations, and suspect our noblest love. There is no hour, even of our weakest and our falsest, when we have not understanding enough for this poor spoiling work; as the common labourer may pull down the church which only genius and skill can raise. But it is not every day, 'tis only the rarest seasons of our life, that can deliver a new and holy image to our souls, to give us silent counsel in temptation, and flit as a light before us in the darkness of our sorrows. Let, then, the spirits of the just remain perfect with us while they may; and let us beware lest, hastily, through the spleen of wilful unbelief, these blessed guests be expelled from our inhospitable hearts.

In the present instance, the truth which stands in the way of our first admiration is of the slenderest kind. No doubt, if all men did their duty, the very materials for self-sacrificing enterprise would scarce remain; and in such a world, the occasion, and, with the occasion, the call to go out beyond the personal bounds on missions of mercy, would appear to cease. If we contribute our individual share for the furtherance of this result, we so far *pay our subscription* towards the golden age that, in bare justice, *men* can demand of us no more; we stand clear of their claims, and, when they come to us with further charges for other men's sins—why then, were we so little *Christians* as to stand upon our strict *rights*, and so little *men* as to be regardless of our social well-being, we might protest against bearing a burden not our own and say, "Go, call them to the reckoning at whose door this evil lies." But it is only as between man and man when God is far away, only in the abstract view of severe distributive justice, that human duty can resolve itself into this mere keeping of accounts; and so little can the moral capital of the world be kept up by this distraining upon bills delivered, that even society and law are perpetually taxing the faithful and orderly to discharge the arrears of the unscrupulous and idle. One half of the machinery and work of all *government* is but the combined effort and outlay of just men to repair the mischiefs of the unjust, and to afford, in the prison, the court, the board of health, the public school, some poor wholesale substitute for individual fidelity. We live in a world in which it is simply impossible to ignore other men's neglected obligations. To look no further than mere self-interest, he who will not own his share in our great company, but insists on keeping separate his particular debtor and creditor account, will only accelerate the ruin which he is so eager to escape. You *cannot* simply let alone the heedlessness and sin at your right hand. If you treat it like dead *chaff* to be just buried out of sight, you will find it all to be living *seed*, that will germinate and spread like the poisonous mangrove, till your habitable lands are turned into a grave. If your neighbour is a sluggard, and allows his garden to run wild, in spite of your protesting justice, your own labour will be increased. At first, perhaps, you will try the effect of greater diligence within the limits of your little plot; you will strengthen its fences; you will ply it with a double weeding power; but the rank grass creeps through the hedge at one end ere you have finished cutting it out at the other; the thistle-down sows its seed with every wind; and in the end you will find it best to take your spade, open your neighbour's wicket while he sleeps, and dig up *his* ground as well as your own. And in the higher view of conscience, this is clearer still. Duty is no fixed, allotted piecework, assigned to us one by one, as if each was on a desert island, and lived a life unaffected by the rest. Rather is it a joint enterprise, a perilous march over the mountain and sharp encounter in the field, committed to us all together, as to an army of the faithful. So when, in this life-battle, the front ranks give way, there is nothing for it but that the second advance to the brunt; and if they too are struck with faint-heartedness and fly, the slighter band in reserve behind must take the risk, and exchange support for conflict; and even though these and every other reliance should prove infirm or faithless, still, unless all is to be lost, some solitary hero of Divine prowess, some leader of faith, some captain of salvation, some Jesus of Nazareth, will hold the desperate field, and, by expostulating death, rally the scattered host, and reopen the hope of victory. There can be no meaner mistake than to suppose that each one's duty remains just what it would be in a world where all performed their part; and only a soul withdrawn from the vivifying look of God, the soul of moral avarice, parsimonious in its expenditure of effort, can delude itself with the imagination that what would save him there can suffice to save him here. Every man, in proportion as he is a true son of the Highest, feels that he *cannot* stand by, seeing misery and guilt within his reach, and say, "It is no concern of mine"; he knows himself responsible for all the wrong *he might prevent,* as well as for all he may *positively do.* Obligation cannot, from its nature, exhaust itself, and come to an end; writing its "Finis," shutting itself up, and standing thenceforth compact and unsuggestive on the shelf. It has no measure but possibility itself, and thus lies ever open for fresh lines of thought and love. Whosoever has received of heaven the suggestion of some practicable deed of goodness or sacrifice of mercy, bears a burthen which he never can lay down, and which will be asked at his hands when he knocks at the everlasting gate. It is the holy trust committed to him; and how is he straitened till it be accomplished! Thus do the special evils of the guilty world make room enough for the special fidelity of saintly minds, and the vast amount of neglected obligation swell the work of faithful men. Nay, not even should we wait for the direct and audible call of God within us. *Without sacrifice* no man will really maintain the spirit of a noble and devout life. And it is well for each to go out deliberately beyond the circle of his apparent personal obligations, and choose for himself some work, just for God's sake alone—some work to which no inclination, no necessity invites him, but which he takes in pure offering to Him. It will help his self-knowledge; it will check his presumption; it will exercise his patience; it will test his fidelity. It is not that such works *constitute* his main duty, and accumulate any gains of merit. They are but like the *timepiece*, which does not *make* our hours, but only *marks* them; yet, by the false measurements it thus prevents, and the self-deceptions it corrects, is a priceless economist of life. So is there no such measurer of the way eternal as the daily sacrifice. As its silent index comes round, the steadiness or trembling of our spirits shows how our reckoning stands with God; and when we feel not its return, save by the passage across our heart of a clearer peace and brighter love, it is no slight indication that our course is ready to be finished, and the hour come that we should be glorified.

www.ingramcontent.com/pod-product-compliance
Lightning Source LLC
Chambersburg PA
CBHW022141160426
43197CB00009B/1376